A PARENT'S LOVE

BY: BERNETTA W. FARMER

LIFE'S GOLDEN TRINKETS PUBLICATIONS

A Parent's Love   sees beyond
limitations.

A parent's love will always be around.

It teaches life lessons that will never let you down.

From the beginning of time a love that last forever.

Messages of encouraging words that will conquer all types of weather.

Just like a newborn child whose life is just beginning

A parent's love nurtures them through as life's wheel starts spinning.

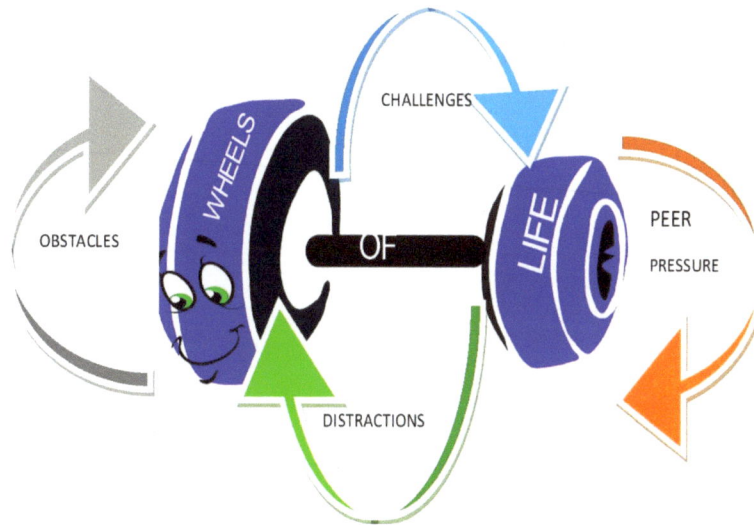

From newborn to toddler love is needed to make them better.

A parent's love to guide them towards the next level.

CHILD

DIRECTION

TO

DESTINY

Parent's Love

This next stage is a crucial one which needs more attention.

Adolescence is the stage that curiousness will be mentioned.

Questions will be asked and statements will be made.

A parent's answer must be carefully thought out so the child will understand.

As the adolescence begin to discover who he or she is,

A parent's love will help guide them through the pain and all the tears.

The principles that a parent give to a child
as they grow older,
It's for them to keep throughout their lives
to cherish and hold on to.

As he or she began to experience the harshness of life.

It's a parent's love that will surely prepare them for the   fight.

A forever love that will always stand the test of time.

A Strong foundation you can depend on Even when the mountain is hard to climb.

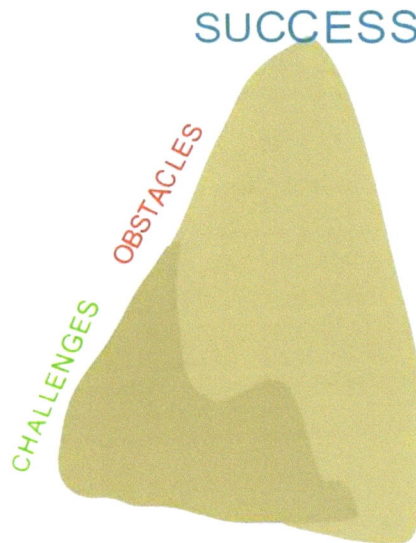

SUCCESS

OBSTACLES

CHALLENGES

Through rain sleet and snow just like the postal service.

A love that delivers on time with gifts that will never hurt us.

PARENT'S LOVE

This is the kind of love that will keep you out of trouble.

Even though it may not seem fair at times.

You will always find it to be rewarding.

A parent's love will protect you

From places that will put you in harm's way.

Trust the direction where it points you to.

It will never lead you astray.

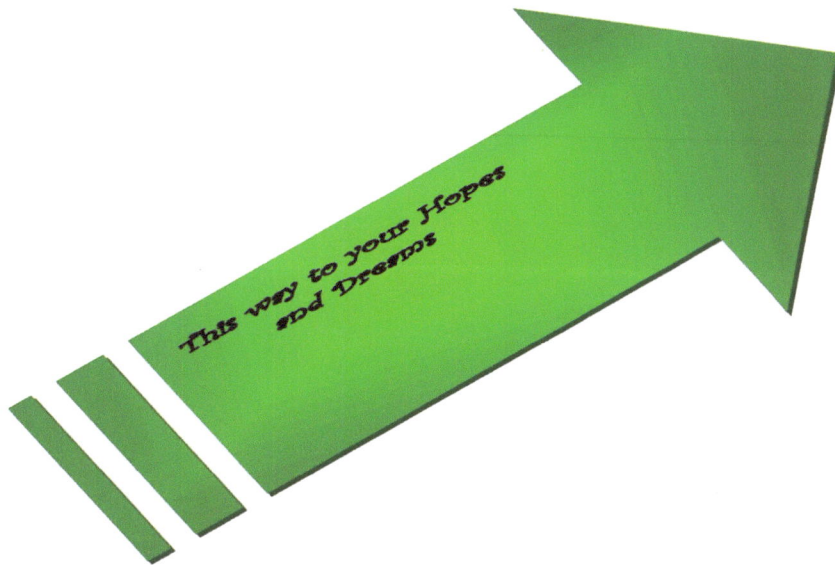

This way to your Hopes and Dreams

Love's not just a temporary feeling.

It will guide you towards destiny.

With every step carefully planned out,

And each day coming closer to your dream.

Like an eagle protects
its' nest,

Love keeps you safe and
sound. Giving strength
where it's needed,

Love will always be around.

17

Just like a tree bearing fruit

So is a parent's love to a child.

Bringing forth truth and knowledge

With wisdom to make you wise.

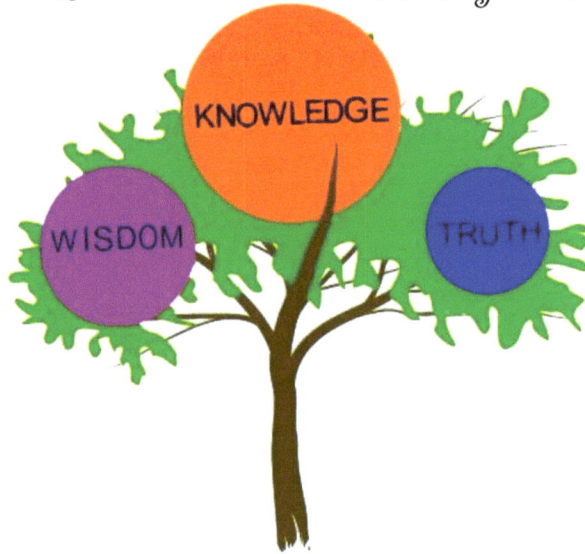

Love will sound off like a trumpet to warn you of dangers beyond.

It's in Love's best interest to keep you safe from harm.

Love will teach you not to worry, be afraid, or have reason to hate.

Your heart and soul were never built for this,

Because your purpose is truly great.

A parent's love is there
when you're all grown up.
For there are questions you may still have
And their love will fill your cup.

For it's the way of a parent
To make sure that you're equipped
In defeating all of life's challenges
When your journey takes you on a ship.

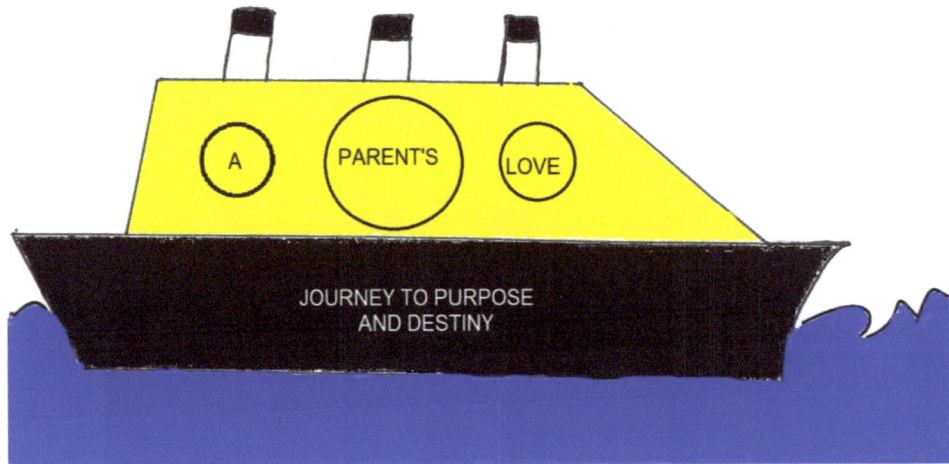

You never want an artificial love or one that is not true.

This kind of love will lead you astray.

So be careful who you lend your ear to.

YOU CAN TRUST ME IM YOUR FRIEND

When it becomes very hard

And there's no one to relate to.

Take a look within your heart.

It's where these words are made true.

A parent's love is a guiding light
To bring hope where you are.
Words of wisdom to fulfill your needs
To take your journey towards the stars.

Hold on to these words of love deep within your heart.

For one day you may need it to share.

With these words one's dreams can go far.

So remember these words of Encouragement.

With them you will surely win.

For this kind of Love will protect you And that you can depend.

A PARENT'S LOVE

Published by: Life's Golden Trinkets Publications

Copyright © 2016
Life's Golden Trinkets Publications
P.M. Box 137
Indianapolis, IN 46250

A Parent's Love
ISBN: 978-0-9893245-0-2

www.ingramcontent.com/pod-product-compliance
Lightning Source LLC
Chambersburg PA
CBHW042118040426
42449CB00002B/86